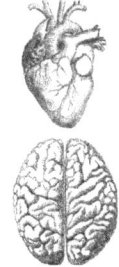

WARNING SHOTS
Peter Faziani

WORDS DANCE PUBLISHING
WordsDance.com

Copyright © Peter Faziani 2017

No part of this book may be used or performed without written consent from the author except for in critical articles & reviews.

1st Edition
ISBN-13: 978-0-9979404-6-6
ISBN-10: 0-9979404-6-8

Cover photograph by Amanda Oaks
Cover design & interior layout by Amanda Oaks
Interior images by Sarah Everett (pp. 26, 28, 46, 60, 64)
          by Amanda Oaks (pp. 36, 38)

Type set in Liberation Serif & Bergamo

Words Dance Publishing
WordsDance.com

For E, who always puts up with me.

WARNING SHOTS
Peter Faziani

I

(13) Willy Wonka Claimed That "Invention, My Dear Friends, Is 93% Perspiration, 6% Electricity, 4% Evaporation, and 2% Butterscotch Ripple," but What About Inspiration?

(15) Cold Steel Stall Walls and ½ Ply Paper: An American Story of Flight

(16) There Are a Finite Number of Times People Can Call You the Fonz Before It Stops Being Funny

(17) Finding Love in All the Wrong Wagons

(19) Bottles and a Relationship on the Verge of Going Nuclear

(20) My Life Is a Creek That Needs a Good Dredging

(22) If You Are the Voice in My Head That's Fine With Me

(23) Romanticizing Minor Memories

(24) A Giant City of Salt Buried 1200 Feet Below the Surface

(25) The Wordsmith Cometh From the Father's Scotch Shadow

(27) When You Figure out a Likely Date of Conception

(29) And There Will Never Be Another Father Like Old Fezziwig

(31) After Zoey, I Question Every Song by Ben Gibbard

(32) I've Got This Friend

(34) Imitation, Flattery, Style, Etc.

(37) Consciousness in Conversation

(39) 71 Words and Kodak Photo Paper

(40) On Writing Poems: A Lesson I Could Learn

(41) If You Give This Man a Megaphone, He'll Probably Read Ginsberg

(42) My Doctor Says the Human Mouth Is Shrinking Because We No Longer Use It Like Our Ancestors

(43) A Little Alka-Seltzer to Help the Day Go Downhill

(44) Roads and Atlases

(45) A Poem That Isn't About Notches in Bedposts or Lines in Songs

(47) The Shore of Lake Michigan Looks Bigger Than the Ocean

(48) I Broke the Emergency Brake Miles Ago and This Is Where We Are Now

(49) Everybody Knows That the Best Way to Describe the Ocean to a Blind Man Is to Push Him In

(50) The Movement's in Motion With Mass Militant Poetry

(51) When Day Drinking Isn't Enough

(52) Hemingway Once Said "Wearing Down Seven Number-Two Pencils Is a Good Day's Work" but When a Cell Phone Buzzes, the Planner Gets Mislaid

(53) Histrionic Personality Disorder Affects More Women Than Men

(54) Let's Keep This Simple: There Are Rules

(55) A Story About Selectively Multitasking

(56) The End of Something Ugly

II

(59) After the Iron Is Gone, I Want to Turn the Slag Into Something Pretty

(61) A Field of View

(62) Sun and Slush

(63) Rooms

(65) Worn and Wearing

(66) Where the Cliffs Meet

(67) Vented Bricks

(68) Moving Air Losing Hair

(69) Stitches

(70) Make Them Fit

(71) And in Closing, I'd Like to Show You All a Mirror of Me

(73) About the Author

(75) Notes + Acknowledgments

WARNING SHOTS

I

Willy Wonka Claimed That "Invention, My Dear Friends, Is 93% Perspiration, 6% Electricity, 4% Evaporation, and 2% Butterscotch Ripple," but What About Inspiration?

A life full of unexamined intertwined moments
except twine is cheap
                frail
                          snaps easy under pressure and
after my 29th birthday I met this poetfriend
a 21st century Whitman
      a real wordsmith
            a dickhead that always has awesome sunglasses
a childhood friend of a friend that I met somewhere else
and I can't help but envy his talent
especially after the last time I read Whitman's "Song of Myself"
      after a few beers I wasn't hearing Whitman's voice
           it was my friend quoting verse at the bar
                counting numbers hastily palmed in ink

he writes poems about his childhood smoke hazed
                              and second hand
last month
      my mother finally told me that I was baptized twice
the first time in Mercy Memorial mere hours postpartum
      doctors didn't think my newborn heart was good enough
                    smart enough
                      strong enough
the second courtesy of St. Pat's Catholic
      I stopped attending weeks after my first Holy Communion

and in the 6th grade
      I loved Ms. Foster more after she returned from Barbados
            as Mrs. Wilson even
though I would never be more than a little Peter in her eyes
I remember that feeling of envy
            rage
                jealousy
building up in my chest after she blushed when a childhood friend
                      offered to catch her if she fell

I guess that it's funny that Ms. Foster taught me that my name
                             means rock

because I've never leaned on anyone more than I lean on her
that pretty Trout Hall resident wearing the jean jacket
                              and fuchsia JanSport back pack

Cold Steel Stall Walls and ½ Ply Paper: An American Story of Flight

I've got this friend who
holds the record for number
of airport bathroom stalls
where a bowel movement has
occurred

Denver & Salt Lake
Pittsburgh & Philadelphia
a whirl-wind clockwise movement

squinting & clenching
straining & sending snaps
his then Snapchat score being upwards of 88,100
he owns his title & dominates his competition
between connecting flights

I wrote this poem in church
waiting for my bread
waiting for some draaaank

I wrote this poem about fifty feet from
the university president
and under twenty-five from an empty cross
suspended from the ceiling

wrote this poem trying
to find a way to integrate the poop
emoji into my poetry

wrote this poem wanting to honor
a friend trying to honor his
beard trying to represent his
Christlike lumbersexuality trying
to cleanse myself
of sin

There Are a Finite Number of Times People Can Call You the Fonz Before It Stops Being Funny

He's clad in armor sewn
from real hand tanned Italian leather
a fashionable black number for men of sophisticated tastes
it's not exactly Arthur Fonzarelli
                          but close

it protects him at home in the states in this veritable war zone of
sex
    booze
        Republicans
and reminds him that
he hasn't been in Europe for nearly a decade

his loosely groomed helmet of coarse brown
beard and hair hides his stressed youthful grimace from
would-be enemies
and when I ask who is Europe
he smirks at my shitty joke

and when our words become clichéd daggers
his armor shields him from those
too jealous to admit it

Finding Love in All the Wrong Wagons

And he first learned the Lord's prayer
Our father and all
Sitting in a cold room lined
with long mismatched folding tables
all with at least one chip in their cheap laminate
uncomfortable steel folding chairs stamped
with an acronym he would eventually come to learn and
loved the revolving number of strange adults
clutching their cigarettes in one hand and a styrofoam cup
of day old coffee in the other
at the time he had yet to try the cigarettes
                                        but his love for coffee
stemmed from an abundance of powdered creamer
and packs upon packs of sweetener
just trying to be one of the guys

there were regulars
people that called to his dad
"hey, Faze, (pronounced like the Muppet Fozzie)
you hanging in there?" but
he was only there for the chicks
for the faux-friendships for the satisfaction
of the court
he counted his sobriety in mandated meetings remaining
a countdown to blast off
a countdown until plastering

Give us this day, our daily bread,

he never heard his dad chant in time
never heard him admit he had a problem
his gums too dry to speak, and a thirst
in need of quenching
never heard him ask for daily bread

when he first learned the Lord's Prayer

forgive us our sin as we forgive others

he learned that of the spiraling cast of characters
about 93% would soon break free
of the wagon's weight

and that his dad has been trailing behind
                                        feet first
                                                for years

Bottles and a Relationship on the Verge of Going Nuclear

He peels labels
from the empty
glass bottles
deep green and dark brown
the calling cards of his memories
too painful to forget

these calling cards cost me
no bottle bill means no dime
and no reason to remember
and every reason to lose it
tossed into the ditch or
overlooked glistening
shattered on the walk
away from the porch

after a three-course meal
prepared together
embracing mixed cultural flavors
and shared casual comments critical
of salty language
and he thinks it's her
and she him
but they'll never reconcile

outside on the sidewalk
the shards glisten
in the moonlight or
rather the shitty yellow
light protecting the property that
invades through the cracks
in her curtains spying as they watch
Hitchcock films snuggled
on the couch

My Life Is a Creek That Needs a Good Dredging

Sabotage
it's not what I do to you
it's what you do you yourself

it's what I've known since age five
as my mother drove her pink Eagle Summit
to a safe house after hastily buckling my sister
and me into the back seat
it's the moment I look back at my home
my father in disgust

it's what I've known since my sixteenth birthday
alone in my bedroom
yellow walled with ceiling trim painted like prison bars
trying to draw friends in for visitation
        platonic or conjugal I just needed someone there

it's all the things I think you're capable of avoiding
she says to me or
I think about you

it's turning the volume up to ten
so I can no longer hear the rumble of trucks
the barking of dogs tied outside so often the grass
becomes a dirt path
the sound of urine splashing against a shoddy garage
just off the alley

it's that fifth case of Bud Light I help load
into my father's 02 Jeep Grand Cherokee in 2013
because he gets a discount for buying in bulk

it's that moment you begin to disregard
the friends that might honestly care
about the mistakes you're making
hand in hand and you begin to hurt me

and it's the moment when I let it happen
because I think I can actually help

it's the moment I want to tell you
that what your dick wants doesn't really matter

but don't because I am afraid to talk shop

it's the moment I realize that my dad was wrong
for being disappointed when I admitted I was still a virgin
that summer at his house in Temperance

it's the moment I stopped writing these things down

If You Are the Voice in My Head That's Fine With Me

My friend's first turntable

more of a record player really
more of a lie
      if I'm being honest

but when we listen to "The Chronic"
he's happy
genuinely happy and not
because he's white and
in the privacy of his own apartment
he gets to sing along when Dre or Snoop
or whomever utters a word I can't say because I'm white too
but because this is a long overdue aural experience

and through a strange train of thought
I'm reminded of an emo song I used to cry to
one where the chorus taught me
"when no one wants you in their life
it's gonna be all right"

and he plays a song for me casually
sipping his whiskey
and though the bottle says bourbon
it's more like rye
waiting for my reaction
eyes fixed on my face and I'm awkward
I don't know what I'm hearing
and I remember that at home I've got a family
that wants me and
here I've got this friendship that needs
some loyalty
after all
I've missed his fucking birthday
for Pete's sake

Romanticizing Minor Memories

PA meets NJ in Italy
a church trip
anything but missionary

the best imitation of love
like a rom-com
moments *Before Sunrise*
Before Sunset
Before Midnight
where all things happen except at best he's
only Ethan Hawke in *Assault on Precinct 13*
not *Dead Poet's Society*
and she's no Julie Delpy

after a fistful of summer Gin & Tonics
opens up about an emotional vacancy
because she's been missing since
she ended the road trips and
long distance phone bills
AT&T's vip customers
and nights on the hood of that old car
after his 17th birthday
under Pennsylvania moonlight in true Hollywood fashion
an infidelity represented in countless
whiskey bottles collected
above kitchen cupboards

dreams of reigniting the recycled heat
back into the monastery hearts
naked beneath the rubble
broken and rebuilt
perfect period architecture
ink tapestries injected
in the walls to hide the scars

A Giant City of Salt Buried 1200 Feet Below the Surface

Too afraid to talk
until he's more than
one Blue Moon in
questionably retelling stories
from one side of the street
yet there's no fault to bear
never cares who I think is
really to blame
never needs to

this friend
is the salt
the earth
the space buried beneath Detroit
                     beneath Pittsburgh
                     beneath some city in Italy
where love has floundered
where he bought a leather jacket

where nostalgia lingers heavy
like the cigarette smoke
from his perpetual last one
and when he smokes a menthol
and coughs out of disgust
I remember the only time I've heard my dad
genuinely laugh

The Wordsmith Cometh From the Father's Scotch Shadow

Wants a father's approval but
just like me
we're judged by a choice in career
and fathers that assume our education
has turned us into Democrat-loving fools
except for his dad is not wholly wrong

like me
he always has one arm hidden
in the glove box to protect those we love
from thieves and fathers and becoming the victims

our fathers tell us stories
tongue loosened and memories freed
from alcohol
remembers screwing all those babes
in Vietnam or worse knowing
that his half-Vietnamese son
never existed or worse was murdered because of
his half-American blood

or accepts blame
for auto accidents beyond his control
and the death of a stranger that is anything
but strange when you think about it

these truths told in confidence but
denied when brought up soberly

fabrications constructed for attention
a history never set down in ink
and my friend is a gunsmith in secrecy

When You Figure out a Likely Date of Conception

A rough thanksgiving conception
    probably punch drunk
    and loveless

arousal by tryptophan and a
bittersweet latticed cherry pie
    except the latticework doesn't stick
    and the Bud Light cans begin to stack up

fast forward three decades
a progenitor's disappointment
in the hormonal choices made
    like college and graduate school
    a lifetime without roughed skin
    dry fingers and torn cuticles

genetical language and he
languishes a father's racialism
in misunderstanding the need to accept cultural
sensitivities
    when correcting—educating
    saying "you can't call people that"
a father's response upends the moment
"you weren't raised like I was. Things were different then."

and he sees his father's eyes flash back
    to father throwing mother
    through the old bay window and
    the police writing it off as a family affair

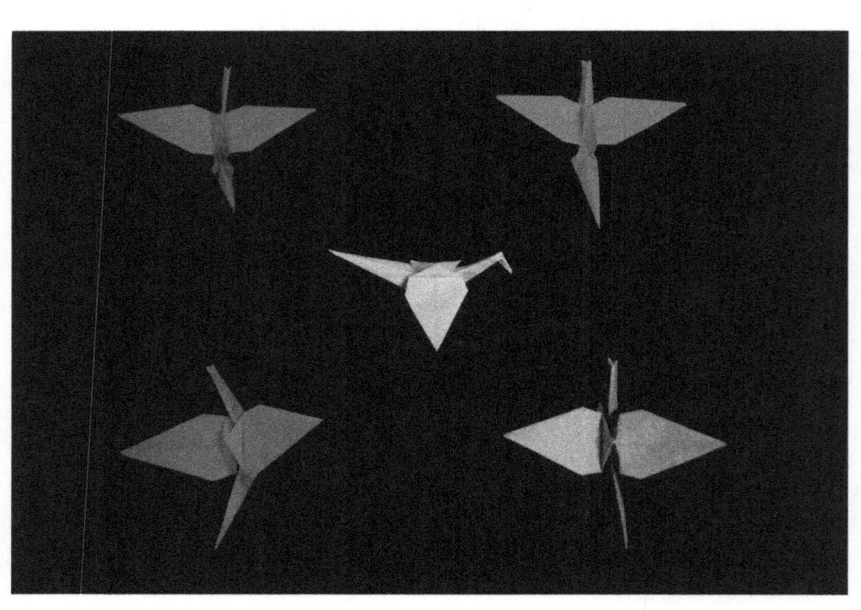

And There Will Never Be Another Father Like Old Fezziwig

I sat down to write a poem about death
for a friend who recently bought his
first funeral suit
    JC Penny
        Black
            Cut
like the suit he wore in their last shared picture
standing next to his grandfather
viscerally carrying his logger's burden

pen to page I've realized that I can't write that poem
since my closest comparable memory
is the narrative my mother tells of me as a two-month-old
under white light in the emotionally dead operating room
watching as I'm laid out on my stomach and an Indian doctor
severs my spare artery

I died twice that day

and plus no one
can write a good poem
about death and dying since
    Shakespeare
        Dickinson
            Poe

I considered writing the poem
to memorialize grandfathers in general
and say tripe about how some grandads
are more like dads and most paps can change
lives but then I realized that it was cliché
and I never knew either of my progenitors
but I've seen pictures of a man on the bow of a boat
smiling a smile missing from the stories

though one can't be sure if he smiled after the cop
let him off after throwing my grandmother through
that bay window

so I decided to write a poem about alcohol

and a poem about my friend's healing process
he prefers Rolling Rock over
Heineken
working class heritage

his Western PA blood chooses
Yeungling and the plastic fibers of his Forever Wallet
are grateful for it
but pitcher after pitcher and
shot after shot
kills the magnet strip
of credit cards

he learned from a young
age to identify a good sipping whiskey
by the genuine cork plugging
the neck of the bottle

he'll raise his glass in honor
to toast or memorialize whenever he's prompted
but more often he'll raise
his thoughts sarcastically
defensively dodging like a bird with a
broken wing

and those thoughts are
always on the rocks

he's got scars

he just got one more

but he's got thick skin
and an ironic mouth
that protects his tumbler
                        bottle
                                  aluminum if money's tight
and to that which we've all lost
my friend knows too
that wounds heal and
in time
with whiskey
he'll be fine

After Zoey, I Question Every Song by Ben Gibbard

Porch drinking late and the sweating bottle
loosens the label
               the tongue
blurs the born-on date
blurs speech
considering the consequences of lighting a smoke
but ashamed for starting
even though it was never no more than a pipe

dizzy standing up to announce plans
to taste some smoke and when
enunciating the French 'une pipe'
she calls him pretentious

reminds her of the Walmart
kitchen mat and its claim that
'Wine is bottled poetry'

alone together
               spiders working diligently
among falling leaves and false distractions
finishing bottles
wondering about former friends
from back home
but they never drank when friends were around
and worse they've moved on without them

I've Got This Friend
for Wes

Broken laces on sole worn shoes
and she dances alone to
a steady rhythm
an old standard
swaying feet still
her fingers beckoning
his dysfunctional self
wearing power line tennies

the band kicks in
manufacturing courage
in a crowded room
fostering fears
in empty intestines
he's been on this wall
for so long he's grown
tendrils to root
into the brick
out of necessity
out of comfort

there's a fishing metaphor
his pap used to say
about casting wide nets
and having lots of sex
but pap was a kook
or at least that's what
he's been lead to believe
yet here he stands
reeling dizzy
to retching because
trees don't move
only sway awkwardly
                    clumsily
during storms or windy days .

eyes connect and everyone is
watching or
at least he feels their eyes
knowing that tree roots unearthed

by tree-spades never survive
he uproots and casts out
insecurities in favor
of a boat load of obvious
false swagger but this
isn't a masquerade ball
an obvious fraud
standing on the feet
of someone much prettier
than he knows how to be

Imitation, Flattery, Style, Etc.

Sewing emotional coat sleeves
internally
infernally
and yet you continue
burning me
serving me
blaming me
saving me
for tomorrow

dust like lingering
lingerie cast
off in a huff
hungry for
horns inserted
but it's casual
imma Ghetto causality
but in her
eyes she sees me
as her General
genitals

broken up
words crafted
from air
rows back she
calls me forward
coming to
explain my pitfalls
elaborate on my
pitiful excuse
for our extraneous
extracurriculars in her
back seat Hummer
she's a rich girl
out of my league
but man is she a bitch girl
busty she ditched me

musty memories
years later
I see her
reunion of old
friends now capsized
oversized and blindsidely
the same
but now she's delivering
for Domino's to pay for
the Infantino buckled into
the backseat
using the tips
to pay for
unexpected deliveries
nine months later
because daddy's
dropped her

Consciousness in Conversation

I keep thinking about the things I need to write down—although I really just need to go to Walmart—I've been thinking about a new water bottle and we're probably low on toilet paper because we're always low on toilet paper—I often find myself checking the mail and hoping for threats—I know I ought to call my mom to catch up on the daily grind but I forgot we need coffee—I spent three hours yesterday thinking about you and Facebook stalking Jackie Chan—I haven't written a poem in months and it's starting to catch up to me—like a cold—or the craving of a nicotine fix—but I'm not sure I have any more cigarettes—and I've still got to—fix the toilet—feed the dog—read that chapter about the Romans—and buy some flip flops for work—ha—my mom calls them floppy flops—I keep remembering all those things I've never acknowledged like the car accident—the shame I felt after losing my virginity—or the time I went vegan—both for the same person—what was her name—I remember finding my dad drunk on the couch with his revolver tucked under his arm—nightmares—flashbacks—PTSD—I always meant to write that down—I always meant to turn that into something he'd be proud of—but I'll never forget how he criticizes me for my education

71 Words and Kodak Photo Paper

Red lights at railroads
and red lights in dark rooms
developing photographs of
dark memories
blurred focal points
mistimed shutter clocks
but in there somewhere
two silhouettes of friendship
soliloquies of secrets
told to each other with the
promise of telling no one else
fueled by the whiskey talking
over the other
with their own ragged truth

On Writing Poems: A Lesson I Could Learn

Bruised and storied and telling stories
better heard aurally
than read textually
bullshit
write it down and edit it
a million yarns to spin
license to poetic
waxing hyperbole
no one questioned Bukowski
so why would they question
you

If You Give This Man a Megaphone, He'll Probably Read Ginsberg

Reads poems to find solace   to confront ghosts of the
space between words between
                       the chars
to hear the echoes and whispers of all the memories
hidden away in an empty breath
weighted down by whiskey
                       menthol
                       and a bruised psyche
tackling a troubled reality
of the punctuating
       and the hesitating

My Doctor Says the Human Mouth Is Shrinking Because We No Longer Use It Like Our Ancestors

Binging on Thai
using chopsticks
in an attempt to slow down
make the digestion worth while
chewing a sparse mouthful
of noodle and chicken
a spicy level ten
claims to be looking for a challenge

doing it to be pretentious
        to hide the shakes
                to hide after a night of long drinking
and double shots of nostalgia

A Little Alka-Seltzer to Help the Day Go Downhill

Swallow words
like pills
painful like pilsner
ooze salt in the
name of a friend
brandishing a needle of ink
wrecked on love
tequila only after heartbreak
whiskey gingerly mixed
with cream into all the AM coffees
and I would've been envious of every
experience in his portfolio
before I met my wife

but my Irish goodbyes openly
offend him
a safety net
from judgement
and being gone
longer than I want

Roads and Atlases

Always carries an atlas
worn and corners creased
heavy from all the roads
that long ago
lost that new map smell

talks of crossing mountains
and the use of condoms
renting condominiums for the night
(never by the quarter of the hour because that's just rude)
to sleep down a B.A.C.
and asserts that he always uses them
as if atlases and condoms
trap the same things

A Poem That Isn't About Notches in Bedposts or Lines in Songs

lies on his back hair sprawled
across 700 thread Egyptian cotton sheets
asking whether Dashboard was wrong

he keeps his hair tightly under control except when
it's not and he's pissed traveling
westward-to-conference
sans hair-tie

stressed he lost his sunglasses
in an Uber
nope
that was me

buys replacement sunglasses weekly
Classic Aviators
          Round
                  Rimless
refuses Clip-Ons out of principle
he's no savage
but never buys his own hair-ties
takes them as trophies

The Shore of Lake Michigan Looks Bigger Than the Ocean

At high tide the shore rakes
the sorrows of the sand clean
a physical act representing
something unattainable
and the memories of the day sink
below the surf to be lost
                      buried
my friend is a lake
he can swallow
a paper ship
or a long emptied bottle

when the ice freezes over
he feels remorse that he couldn't
go home for the holidays
because who invites the lake
in for Christmas Ham?

he feels even worse come spring
when animals sprung
trek out on the ice
paying no mind to the cracks
racing alongside the paw prints
a deadly trap of the lake
raking in the tail

I Broke the Emergency Brake Miles Ago and This Is Where We Are Now

With microphone in hand he brushes strays from his face
insults from shoulders and plays everything so cool
when alcohol's involved and women are on the table

singing for the attention but the details get lost in the karaoke muzak
prefers brown hair and heavy rimmed glasses are a plus
but anyone'll probably get the job

believes all women fawn and he readily tries to fall in love but
they're really just a Bukowskian safety net
a defense mechanism to create false normalcy

but when the whiskey sloshes out of the glass and
runs down his hands I can see the sadness and loss in his eyes because
he's jealous of his own knuckles

Everybody Knows That the Best Way to Describe the Ocean to a Blind Man Is to Push Him In

Mattress mate ghosts
and a growing pile of underthings
closet living

a bottle becomes the key
        a bottle or two or three
to a night of hard living and a day
of poor sleep and 3:46 AM text message arguments

whose job is it to intervene
when he's locked himself in a bottle
and is drifting alone at sea?

who's to blame if he sinks in the deep end?
the ocean is a salty place and his salinity
rises in relationship to the sanity of his blanket
distribution
        a balled up mess avoiding the black light

personal responsibility teaches me that it's not my job
to put out the lit cannon fuse smoldering and tied to his
Christlike beard
        a modern Edward Teach plundering the boats
and beds as the fuse
burns a path toward a powder keg of
memories of curly brown hair buried deep in his hippocampus

and I can't help but feel that if I could have only stopped my father
        like he'd stop his father
I could crack the bottle
and free the ghosts inside
glass too green to understand that some fears run deeper
than some sand faults

The Movement's in Motion With Mass Militant Poetry

Pledges an uphill attack like Sisyphus
a hierarchical blood bath
slaying the powerful on top
in the name of everyone on the bottom
blind to the consequence
that blood pools at the lowest point

already staining dimpled chins and rising
to Noahatic flood levels
his balsa pen is holding up
like granite
        his ink flowing
his words sewing the discontent
of a malcontent that curses too much

When Day Drinking Isn't Enough

Drunk early   brown glass night light bottle
tip throat down throw   done shattered
shard friends shared fist fight
fiend food find burger fries
                            five   girl pretty blonde brown red maybe
dark
      number six digits palm green   smudged temporary tattoo

drink up free hands passing over
                        dance gyrate shake
                                        wake up to blue

                                          and hair alone

Hemingway Once Said "Wearing Down Seven Number-Two Pencils Is a Good Day's Work" but When a Cell Phone Buzzes, the Planner Gets Mislaid

Text message reads
    formal
        a Q&A   keeping
it professional
        "You busy later?"
"When?"
    "3:00?"
"How's 3:30?"

no pretense
    well
        not really

    puts a record on
for show
demonstrating a refined taste in music
where Dre sets the mood

it's casual
    caustic
        socially hazardous
so try to keep it secret
    code names
        Ms. Big
            Mr. Little

like all good erections
this'll all blow
soon
    right in someone's face

Histrionic Personality Disorder Affects More Women Than Men

Addicted to attention
sexual amphetamines
through phallic syringe
injected into others

public confidence carries
ghosts riding sidesaddle
down tired spines
bagging bottles
ladies practically begging

digits and members
numbers and rank

mimics learned behaviors
rose coloured bloody sheets missing
from the windowsill
deals long sealed
Hail Mary long forsaken

gabbing on and on
incessant speech
about work put in
and tolls taken out

Let's Keep This Simple: There Are Rules

Wants the D.C. long game
but plays the Indiana barely aged short game
MVP of everything but std
or sti
        or stopping

options like out of focus raindrops
on a windshield of life
every drop reflects a different
image
a memory nostalgic
of moments lost better yet
Amandonded

I'm not sure there's ever been an Amanda

but I've known one or two myself

lives life as a consequence
of what can be seen
instead of that which can't
and it causes trouble

sees things as a binary instance
unattached feelings of attractive
Constance

I'm also not sure there's ever been a Constance

but there's an age that passes

old enough to know bitter
and beyond staying friends

that hasn't passed yet

A Story About Selectively Multitasking

Can't handle two browser tabs
       without rising blood pressure
       and anxious drops of cheek sweat
but dates
er sleeps
er call it like it is
fucks
       2 or 3 or 4 girls at a time

unfilled slots
       in a yearly planner
but claims to be too busy
       because Imgur can't wait and
       an orgasm equates the end
       of the work day
       some time around noon

The End of Something Ugly

A bloody nose
      draining like
friendships quartered
drawn tight like skin
mere hours post Botox

red rockets burst over
ripped up bedclothes
      anger not semen
on the hunt for digits
a bot to text bawdily
          bodily
someone to emotionally engage
someone to ultimately
          compromise

and when that body
is finally erased
      from her contact list
angrily denies any culpability

II

After the Iron Is Gone, I Want to Turn the Slag Into Something Pretty

Unquenchable thirst to
help others
dig the trenches
in unmapped lives

on death
commands no mourning
or experiences hardened
into memories
plottable on worn maps

of the faces of family

of heart opening to help

or the blues of her eyes

no slow dances
no soft tears—

pack your fucking bags
and hit the road
in his memory

and if he's done his job
a part of him will always
go traveling too

A Field of View

Imagines the future
                any given day
sitting with her
resting on a salt worn
wooden porch swing
clutching finger tips
wrinkled with age
as gray skies are cast off

jealous of the breeze
blowing strands of still
beautiful hair each slow gust rocks
back and forth as they end
the twenty-seven thousandth sunset
looking out from a deck
onto the space where the sand meets
the water and where the water
meets the sky
a deck that's long
overdue for a good staining

but hopes for a good laugh
as her cheeks rose red
from finally finishing that bottle of
Traverse City Riesling before chugging
more than a fair share

biggest regret is not opening a bottle
with her sooner
.

Sun and Slush

Sam Adams Cherry Wheat
the first beer he could stomach
carried a sixer to the apartment volleyball court
hoping to chat up the ladies
because beer made everyone cooler
but never drank to be cool

he believed that
only alcoholics drank alone
on the porch
in the garage
at the bar
all hours of the day
tucked away from the sun

instead of tucking in their son

father told him to work hard
and sitting on the sidelines
sun drunk and dizzy
other men made the jokes and got the digits
realized ten years later he needed to work sober not hard
and it must have been a limited
application because he never
took his own advice

Rooms

Father lived away
in multiple war
worn rooms of marriage
conscripting a new bat-man each time

inviting son
into a green zone
within father's compromised
airspace choked
with secondhand serenades
screaming from the balcony

or slamming down
bottles and doors
until she waved the white flag
and father waived his rights
and radioed the cheapest lawyers

away from the front
miles behind the lines
son listened to a childhood father's wallet paid for
on cassettes and cds
a playlist of albums from father's childhood
in son's room like another country
on a single disc player bought for him
and son wondered what it was
like being a father like you

father was torn
by his age and memories
and a son interested in poetry and
never had a picture of the enemy
never knew it by sight
but the shit was always outside father's room
when he lived away

Worn and Wearing

He hopes she never
tires of him
because he's the lucky one
and she's got little
to show for in him

Where the Cliffs Meet

When was the last time he
slept through the night?
it's like they're both infants
needing a mother

a desert landscape
of tears flooded
with noise
and he can't comprehend
relationship problems on
two hours of REM-less sleep

And when his head finally hits the pillow
a mechanical switch flips and he's out
craving the time he gets
before sunrises long hidden
by trees and mountains

Vented Bricks

Can't hear
temper in
any voice but
yours
      your anger and pain
           your suffering
unacknowledged

and I know that they
can even hear it carry over into mine
        exasperated voice cracks
        into breathless sighs

healing is in their
compassionate tones
      and comforting bright blue eyes and soft
forgiving voices

and I'm sorry that you're hardened
beyond a healing
      and that I haven't been
able to break through into you
to help heal

Moving Air Losing Hair

Working
odd hours and
little sleep
is worth it
knowing she's
tucked in comfortably
under the loose-leaf papers
and shambolic sheets

wonders if there's still time to find her
once he's made a difference
in the world that a family could
be proud of
even if he's only
a figment of once
grand plans and
missed expectations

can they still share
green mountains and orange sunrises
sandy beaches and blue waters
where he wants to tell her how pretty
she's become
and she'll blush
like red leaves falling in autumn?

Stitches

Unforgettable moments in broken fragments
like breaking irons into rapiers
long forgotten dangers of doing stupid things

six years old

winning wars

touring Mars

and he can't get back there

and he can't reinvent it

history leveled into broken bricks
shattered glass and one of the many times he went to the ER

Make Them Fit

A mistake of his own
a product of poor decisions
and parental absences
an action comprised of inactions
unconvincingly failing

can't even pull off screwing up
without angry wolf memories
commanding "Think before you talk"
or a mother's slow drawl
affirming everyone else's jealousy

but those books on his shelves
the ones with spines
the ones that go uncreased
tell him to keep struggling
to put one word
in front of the other foot
on and on and on
blood and spit
into ink and pulp.

And in Closing, I'd Like to Show You All a Mirror of Me

Extract from me this venomous
defense mechanism working in tandem
with my false lyricist cooing
an echo haunted by baby's breath
and vipers milk
      I swear it's a necessity in this profession

cutting and copying
      real life and realer people
clipping and coping
      imagination and false niceties
all bound together into one still life
where we become caricatures
with fangs for k-9s

and when I look into my mirror
I know it's never been you
but me

the venom is me

ABOUT THE AUTHOR

Peter Faziani is currently working on his PhD at Indiana University of Pennsylvania and is also the general editor of Red Flag Poetry. Previously, his poems have been published in *Words Dance*, *The Rising Phoenix Review*, *Ocean State Review*, *The Collagist*, *Sandy River Review*, *Silver Birch Press*, *The Tau* among others. He is a Michigander at heart living in Western Pennsylvania with his family and two boisterous corgis where they enjoy hiking and being out of doors.

NOTES + ACKNOWLEDGMENTS

I would like to acknowledge the following people for the all-around inspirational qualities that make them the fantastic human beings that they are, Wesley Scott McMasters, Matt Stumpf, John Dorsey, and Amanda Oaks. Additionally, without the help and guidance of such an amazing press that is *Words Dance*, this project would've been buried in the figurative bottom drawer of my computer. Additional thanks go out to Sarah Everett for her help in the design and editing of several of the included photographs, as well as Emily McMichael for her work in creating the beautiful pieces of origami in several of the photos. Furthermore, I would like to thank AJ Schmitz for his suggestions in the editing process. Finally, the wonderful cover designed by Amanda Oaks wouldn't be possible without the help of Jordan from Spaghetti Benders.

"Roads and Atlases published as "I've Got This Friend #8 (Roads and Atlases)" in *Ocean State Review*

"When Day Drinking isn't Enough" first published as "I've Got This Friend #12" in *Words Dance*

"After Zoey, I Question Every Song by Ben Gibbard" first published in *New Growth Arts Review*

Earlier versions of "Finding Love in all the Wrong Wagons and Stitches" first published in *Rising Phoenix Review*

An earlier version of "71 Words and Kodak Photo Paper" titled "71 Words and Photopaper" was published in 2017 issue of *The Tau*

"After the Iron is Gone," "I Want to turn the Slag into Something Pretty," "A Field of View," "Sun and Slush," "Rooms," "Worn and Wearing," "Where the Cliffs Meet, "Vented Bricks, "Moving Air Losing Hair" all originally appeared as part of a small group titled *A Field of View* that took its inspiration from the 2013 album of the same name by The Caber Toss. Check them out.

"Everybody Knows That the Best Way to Describe the Ocean to a Blind Man Is to Push Him In" is a line borrowed from "Everyone is Dressed Up" off American Football's LP2 (2016)

"If You Are the Voice in My Head That's Fine With Me" is a line borrowed from "Everything Starts Where It Ends" from Lovedrug's Everything Starts Where It Ends (2007)

"The Movement's in Motion With Mass Militant Poetry" is a line borrowed from Rage Against the Machine's "Take the Power Back" from Rage Against the Machine (1992)

WORDS DANCE PUBLISHING has one aim:

To spread mind-blowing / heart-opening poetry.

Words Dance artfully & carefully wrangles words that were born to dance wildly in the heart-mind matrix. Rich, edgy, raw, emotionally-charged energy balled up & waiting to whip your eyes wild; we rally together words that were written to make your heart go boom right before they slay your mind.

Words Dance Publishing is an independent press out of Pennsylvania. We work closely & collaboratively with all of our writers to ensure that their words continue to breathe in a sound & stunning home. Most importantly though, we leave the windows in these homes unlocked so you, the reader, can crawl in & throw one fuck of a house party.

To learn more about our books, authors, events & Words Dance Poetry Magazine, visit:

WORDSDANCE.COM

Titles from
WORDS DANCE PUBLISHING

Crybaby by Caitlyn Siehl
No Matter the Time by Fortesa Latifi
Why I'm Not Where You Are by Brianna Albers
Before the First Kiss by Ashe Vernon & Trista Mateer
Our Bodies & Other Fine Machines by Natalie Wee
Trying to Be a Person by Wesley Scott McMasters
When Minerva's Knees Hit the Ground by Amanda Oaks
A Field of Blooming Bruises by Schuyler Peck
To Break the Heart of the Sun by William Taylor Jr.
Where'd You Put the Keys Girl by Amanda Oaks
The War on Unicorns by Brian James Dawson
The No You Never Listened To by Meggie Royer
Dowry Meat by Heather Knox
Chloe by Kristina Haynes
Belly of the Beast by Ashe Vernon
Shaking the Trees by Azra Tabassum
SparkleFat by Melissa May
What We Buried by Caitlyn Siehl
Love and Other Small Wars by Donna-Marie Riley
What To Do After She Says No by Kris Ryan
No Glass Allowed by Tammy Foster Brewer
Nothing Unrequited Here by Heather Bell
The Map of Our Garden by Rebecca Schumejda
Fossil Fuels by Jessica Dawson
I Eat Crow + Blue Collar at Best by Amanda Oaks + Zach Fishel
Literary Sexts Volumes 1 + 2 : Short & Sexy Love Poems
Poem Your Heart Out Volume 1: Poems, Prompts & Room To Add Your Own

DO YOU WRITE POETRY?
Submit it to our biweekly online magazine!

We publish poems every Tuesday & Thursday on website.

Come see what all the fuss is about!

We like Poems that sneak up on you. Poems that make out with you. Poems that bloody your mouth just to kiss it clean. Poems that bite your cheek so you spend all day tonguing the wound. Poems that vandalize your heart. Poems that act like a tin can phone connecting you to your childhood. Fire Alarm Poems. Glitterbomb Poems. Jailbreak Poems. Poems that could marry the land or the sea; that are both the hero & the villain. Poems that are the matches when there is a city-wide power outage. Poems that throw you overboard just dive in & save your ass. Poems that push you down on the stoop in front of history's door screaming at you to knock. Poems that are soft enough to fall asleep on. Poems that will still be clinging to the walls inside of your bones on your 90th birthday. We like poems. Submit yours.

WORDSDANCE.COM

www.ingramcontent.com/pod-product-compliance
Lightning Source LLC
Chambersburg PA
CBHW051701040426
42446CB00009B/1245